A side hustles what you should know:

How to Be Successful in Your Side Hustle

Gift Lawrence

All rights reserved. No part of this publication may be reproduced, distributed, or transmitted in any form or by any means, including photocopying, recording, or other electronic or mechanical methods, without the prior written permission of the publisher, except in the case of brief quotations embodied in critical reviews and certain other noncommercial uses permitted by copyright law.

Copyright © Gift Lawrence, 2023.

Table of contents

Chapter 1: A Side Hustle: What Is It? Including Benefits And Examples

Chapter 2: What to consider before beginning a side business While planning a side hustle

Chapter 3: How to Make Your Side hustle Successful

Chapter 4: Preparations You Should Make Before Making Your Side hustle a Full-Time Business

Chapter 5: How to locate a qualified business mentor.

Chapter 6: Reasons Why Every Entrepreneur Needs A Mentor, Regardless Of Success

Chapter 1: A Side Hustle: What Is It? Including Benefits And Examples

A Side Hustle: What Is It?
You can select a suitable second job with the aid of knowing the definition of a side hustle. In addition to your full-time employment, you also have a side business. A side hustle offers greater independence and control than part-time employment because it allows an individual to decide what they do, how much they work, and when they work it. Supplemental income is made possible by the side business. Because they present prospects for a career change, these side occupations are appealing.

You can even turn your second job into a full-time chance if it offers you the opportunity to make a large salary. Making a side job your main source of income involves strategy and investigation. Surprisingly, having a second job enables you to network with people from all backgrounds, enter the world of entrepreneurship, and engage in freelance work.

What Benefits Do Side Jobs Offer?
Having a second job offers the benefits listed below:

optimizing your finances
A strategy to augment a full-time job's pay is by working a side hustle. It might be simpler to pay off debt, purchase luxuries, or build your savings with the added extra money. Your side business could quickly develop into a flourishing enterprise with the additional money.

Making accommodations for flexibility at work
Having flexibility about working hours and freedom at work is another benefit of having a second job. There isn't always a supervisor because most side jobs are self-employed endeavors. Your schedule of employment is up to you. You may be inspired to succeed at work by this flexibility.

seeking out your passion
Many people frequently integrate their passion into their side business to make it profitable. You can even make a career out of following your love. Exploring your interest may help you to develop particular talents.

building up your talent and creativity
Your creativity will grow and be channeled, which is another benefit of doing a second job. You can test your imagination, for example, if you take up graphic design as a side business. Additionally, it gives you the chance to develop a certain skill set, which could progress your career.

Case Studies Of Side Businesses
You can work these extra jobs in addition to your regular job, which is listed below:

Caregiver
If you enjoy working with small children, becoming a caregiver can be a rewarding career.

Playing with the kids, feeding them, helping them with their schoolwork, and keeping them on a regular sleep schedule are the key responsibilities of this employment. When you give excellent care
to children, you may effectively grow this job through word-of-mouth advertising. Some parents may need assistance while they drop their kids off at your house for business meals.

Tutor
A lot of kids who are enrolled in school need additional assistance with their coursework and studies. A lucrative side business could be providing teaching in a subject of your choosing. Either in person or online, you can provide this service. Because you only instruct during the evenings and weekends, this side business typically allows you to hold down a full-time position.

Copywriter

You can aid clients with material by working as a freelance copywriter, which is another profitable side job. Your main responsibility as a copywriter is to provide engaging content that informs your audience about worthwhile goods and services while promoting those goods and services. You can write for one or more clients at once while also writing for websites, blogs, advertisements, articles, and social media posts.

Web developer

A web designer is a member of the information technology industry who creates the structure, aesthetics, and usability of websites. Using their design and technical skills, they develop websites that are both aesthetically pleasing and useful. Your duties as a web designer may occasionally include website upkeep and updating.

Internet marketer

As a side business, affiliate marketing focuses mostly on promoting goods and services through content. As an affiliate marketer, you collaborate with a company and be paid a commission based on how many people you send their way to the website. Typically, there is no cost to join an affiliate network, so starting your second career does not need a big financial commitment. You can generate respectable revenue through affiliate marketing, depending on your chosen marketing strategies.

A disc jockey
During occasions like weddings, engagements, or parties, a disc jockey or DJ works weekends or late shifts. Although this side business offers the potential for substantial revenue, juggling it with a full-time job can be difficult. The sound equipment needed for this side business must be purchased. A successful DJ profession also requires a love of music and an ongoing interest in the newest tracks.

professional photographer
A freelance photographer is another popular side hustle. You can snap pictures at events like

weddings and other gatherings if you decide to pursue this as a side business. You can work with one client and meet their needs. As a freelance photographer, you have the freedom to select the kind of work and reject assignments that do not suit your interests or photographic style. If you attract more clients, you could even be able to make this side business your full-time job.

Virtual helper
For a small business owner, a virtual assistant serves as an administrative assistant. These helpers are remote workers. They assist business owners with trip preparations, appointment scheduling, presentation creation, budget management, and phone support. In addition to these tasks, an employer could ask them to finish other tasks depending on the business and industry.

Influencer
Influencer marketing is a fun and rewarding side business. An influencer uses social media to

interact with their audience and provide valuable material for them. To engage the target audience, you can share amusing videos and memes or advertise a product. You can earn money as an influencer through affiliate relationships, sponsored content, and adverts. Building this hustle might take a little longer, even though it is a lucrative career alternative.

Tutor in life
A life coach is a wellness expert who supports clients in realizing their full potential and achieving their objectives in life. Using their coaching abilities, these professionals identify barriers and devise plans for both personal and professional growth. They aid people in achieving success in a variety of domains, including business, relationships, and marketing. Through constant support and frequent gatherings, they foster a more balanced life. A life coach helps their clients by giving them unbiased support.

decorator of interiors

A specialist that works with clients to enhance a home's interior design and aesthetic appeal is known as an interior decorator or designer. They visit with clients to learn about their needs, preferences, and house designs. To match a room, workplace, or home, a portion of their job entails selecting paint colors, furniture, textiles, and accessories.

pet stylist

A pet groomer is a fun side business to have. These experts offer cleaning and styling services, including bathing, pet grooming, and style fur. These experts could work for kennels, pet shops, and private grooming services. Pet groomers frequently operate as independent contractors and travel to different locations to meet with their clients.

Travel advisor

Travel consultants are experts who arrange trips and vacations for organizations, people, and groups. A travel consultant differs from a travel agent in that they put more emphasis on comprehending a client's needs while also contributing to the company's bottom line. These experts frequently offer unique travel suggestions and aid in locating the most affordable travel options.

tour director

Professionals serve as tour guides, escorting groups of tourists around cities, villages, and museums. A tour guide gathers knowledge about numerous historical locations and imparts it to tourists. For the sake of the tour group's experience, they describe various works of art and artifacts. Professionals may serve as tour guides on the weekends or beyond regular business hours. Along with regular compensation, this side business might also provide extra tips.

Chapter 2: What to consider before beginning a side business While planning a side hustle

A wonderful approach to boost your savings, pay off debt, save for a particular goal, or give yourself some more wiggle space in your monthly budget is to consider starting a side business. But there are a few things you should know before you start if you want to establish a side business, and it all starts with a strategy.

Plan ahead and set goals.

There are numerous different kinds of side businesses. The list appears to go on forever and keeps expanding. Therefore, think about your specific objectives rather than making a list of all the other side jobs you may do. Do you wish to work on your side business temporarily or permanently? What are your ambitions, and how much money will it take to accomplish them?

Take Your Interests Into Account

Consider your hobbies in addition to your ambitions. If you pick a side business that you currently enjoy or are interested in, you'll appreciate it more. Possibly a pastime? There are numerous additional options besides that one. Think about your present abilities, expertise, and experience as well. Then look into how and where you may use your talents to meet needs in your neighborhood or online.

Remember that you can work your side gig locally or virtually depending on the type of work you select.

Make a Time Investment Plan.

Considering how much time you have to dedicate to your side business is another factor. Some side jobs take more time than others to complete. Some develop into full-time occupations later on. Some continue to be temporary or part-time positions.

If you already have a full-time job, think about what other commitments and duties you have that can conflict with your side business. Knowing how much time you can devote to your side business without going overboard will help you avoid overcommitting and establish a timetable that works for you.

What Financial Investment Do You Have?

Depending on the side hustle, you may need to spend in your business to get it started, to keep it going, to keep your talents sharp, and to preserve your competitive edge. Any firm, including side businesses, must make this investment. You'll face some rivalry in the market, just like other companies. To differentiate yourself from the competition, you'll need to invest in yourself, but be careful not to overdo it while your company is still in its infancy and during the pre-launch or launch phases. Consider whether you have an immediate need for it for your business or whether it can wait a little while. Keep in mind that your side business should help you earn money.

Promote Your Company for Success

You must promote your side business if you want to succeed, but you don't have to spend a lot of money on an expensive campaign while you're just starting. If your side business starts to generate more money, you might want to think about running a campaign.

Start with advice on organic marketing for now. In other words, promote oneself in ways that are inexpensive or free. Make use of social media to your benefit. Create a blog and discuss your goods or services, why people might need them, and provide helpful advice on the issues they might solve. To draw readers in and keep them engaged, create value, and keep things interesting. Also, keep in mind that gaining a following takes time. Success rarely occurs overnight.

network within your neighborhood. Don't be hesitant to get in touch with people who match your potential client's profile, but before, do your homework. The effort is more, but the reward can be bigger.

Set realistic financial goals.

Set realistic goals for the amount of money you want to make when you first start. Even a side venture requires time to launch. As your firm expands, it is still possible for it to be profitable and successful, just like other commercial endeavors.

Don't forget your savings as you start to make money from your side gig. This advice is essential, especially if you decide to turn your side business into a full-time endeavor later on. As a result of the ebb and flow nature of side hustle revenue, you should prepare for those periods. Additionally, you should prepare for times when the market is erratic. If you plan to turn your side gig into a full-time career in the future, aim to increase your emergency funds to cover 9 to 12 months' worth of costs. If not, try to save enough money to last for three to six months.

If you want to keep up your side business for a long time, you need also to open a business savings account. Your self-employment taxes, any insurance you might require, such as professional liability insurance, any equipment or subscriptions you might need, as well as upskilling, will all be covered with the aid of this account, among other necessities. A business account can give you an advantage during tax season by making it simpler to see what expenses you might be able to deduct and how much income you made. It also helps you keep business income separate from personal income.

The key to your success is keeping track of your earnings, spending, and business financing.

Regardless of what your goals are, starting a side business will help you get there faster. It takes a lot of work to start a side business, but you don't have to do it by yourself. Partner with Extraco Banks for your company's financial requirements, and allow us to support your aspirations.

Chapter 3: How to Make Your Side hustle Successful

Is selling protein shakes your calling? Does it involve making homemade, gluten-free dog treats? Your passion is whatever it is that you often think about and wish you could do for a living. You might not have the luxury of choosing something you are passionate about if your day job isn't providing for your needs, but ideally, you can at least locate something that interests you. You might not be able to charge $1,000 per painting, but you could start an Etsy store and offer prints or other unique products. By picking a hobby you enjoy, you'll be more likely to persist with it when you grow bored and it won't feel like work. Make things fun, even if it's not necessarily your passion.

Control your time.

I find it challenging with this one. A lot. My blog originally began as a side business.

Technically, I don't earn a full-time living from it (yet), but I'm getting there. Unfortunately, I don't use my time well, so it tends to eat up an excessive amount of it. Social media causes me to lose focus, get sidetracked on Pinterest, and become ineffective. Even though social media IS a component of blogging, it takes up more of my time than it should. You may still enjoy your free time if you don't let your side business take over your life by managing your time.

Make the effort worthwhile.

A side hustle must generate revenue to be distinguished from a hobby. You are wasting your time if you want to sell Lularoe because you love their product but you are only making an average of $2 per hour because the market is saturated and you aren't excellent at sales. Keep doing it unless you want to make selling leggings your pastime rather than a successful side business. But if you want to make money, you must decide how much your time is worth and refuse to accept anything less.

You must occasionally cut your losses.

This holds not just for the MLM community but also for other side businesses. Don't be scared to leave if you find yourself "in too deep" and you aren't producing money after a fair amount of time. I've heard of a lot of people joining these direct sales opportunities and then saying, "Well, I can't resign since I already paid $1000, but then I have to buy fresh inventory which is another $500." STOP if it isn't working within the allotted time. Cut your losses, then proceed. Don't keep pouring money into a ship that is sinking. Feel no obligation to remain. Give it your best go, but don't continue doing something that will cost you more money than it will bring in, and certainly don't continue doing anything you detest.

Avoid getting burned out

This is arguably the most crucial aspect of having a successful side business. Being a solopreneur or entrepreneur can quickly result in burnout, especially if you're working another full- or part-time job on top of your side gig (or have a house full of kids you're responsible for). Make sure you schedule time for yourself and prioritize self-care by keeping a self-care kit on hand and using it. Take a moment to breathe; it's not a luxury, it's a necessity. Don't feel bad about it.

Keeping in mind why you started your side business

Some people establish a side business intending to eventually quit their day job to focus exclusively on it. Some people start a side business because their primary or full-time employment doesn't cover their expenses. No matter why you started, keep in mind your motivation. In the second case, it's less about realizing your dream and more about keeping the lights on. Keep the dream and the end in mind. Simply maintaining your current level of existence is a perfectly acceptable objective; just keep in mind that this is only a means to an end.

Remind yourself to say "thank you"

This does relate to what I stated before about taking care of oneself, but what's more essential is that you need to periodically stand back and give yourself credit for kicking ass. You are stepping up to the plate and giving it your all, which is more than many individuals can say for themselves. Even if you feel like you're failing because you're still succeeding in your side business, YOU are a badass and you should be proud of yourself, whether you're doing it for yourself, your spouse, or your family. Keep your chin up, tell yourself you are fantastic and know that things will improve.

Chapter 4: Preparations You Should Make Before Making Your Side hustle a Full-Time Business

Your scenario and if you've made enough money to replace what you make at your day job, or at least enough to pay your expenses, will frequently determine whether you can transition your side business into a full-time position. Along with adding diversity to your life, side jobs can help you pay off student loans or earn extra cash through passive income.

These ten stages will enable you to advance your successful side business to the point where it becomes your primary source of income.

Here are 10 measures to follow to convert your side business into a full-time venture:

1. Make a plan.

The first step in planning to take your side work full-time is to draft a business plan. Your company's objectives and your strategy for achieving them are laid out in a business plan. It also explains other facets of your company, such as marketing, sales forecasts, and your current financial situation. A company plan paints a detailed picture of your current situation and desired future course. It can assist in keeping you organized, accountable, and on track, just like any excellent strategy.

2. Understand numbers

Revenue and company metrics are important figures to take into account while starting a business full-time. You should first make sure that your company makes enough money to pay its costs and more. Once you make the switch to full-time, you should ideally see a quick boost in your business income, but there is no assurance of this. Create a sizeable emergency fund to take care of yourself in case something goes wrong.

Business owners also need to have a firm grasp of their company's financial parameters, such as sales, costs, profits, and cash flow. You may better plan for future decisions by knowing and comprehending your business's financial data.

3. Clarify the "why"

It's okay if your side hustle first served as a means of earning some extra money. But it might need a little more thinking if you want to make it your full-time job. Why do you want to develop your company further? Is it because you enjoy your job? Is it to give yourself or your family a better life? Your company's "why" is equally as significant as its "what" and "how."

Like many business owners, you can run into a wall or overextend yourself, which will lead to burnout. Understanding your motivations can keep you focused when things get difficult and prevent burnout.

4. Recognize your industry and clientele
There is a distinction between generating additional revenue and relying solely on a legitimate business for your livelihood. You must comprehend the market to build a business that resonates with clients. By conducting market research and examining your competitors, you can find out more about your market. What are they doing well? And what would you change?

Any successful business relies on its customers to survive. Use affiliate marketing, social media, adverts, and, if your client base is sufficiently vast, community development as a means of connecting with your present and potential customers. Learn about the issues they encounter and devise solutions.

5. Begin modestly
You hardly ever come across a business owner who has become successful overnight. It typically takes time to turn an idea into a profitable business. Starting small is perfectly

acceptable, especially when acquiring new abilities.

If you're a freelancer, for instance, you can start modestly on websites like Upwork and Fiverr. These websites may not pay you much money, but they can aid in the development of your resume. Get started, invest the time necessary to grow your firm, and then move on to clients who will pay you more.

The same is true for advertising your company. With so many social media outlets at your disposal, it could seem like a smart idea to spread the word about your company everywhere. Even after working full-time, it might be difficult to successfully advertise yourself across all platforms. Choose one or two social media platforms to grow and worry about the others later.

6. Establish goals for your company
Spend some time creating goals for your company. Think about the goals you want to

achieve in terms of revenue, sales, or other milestones. Set attainable goals in writing so you can monitor your progress.

Likewise, keep your objectives straightforward. Start with three to five objectives, both short-term and long-term. Goals should be written down and kept visible to serve as a regular reminder. Regularly review your goals and make any necessary adjustments.

7. Maintain order in your company's finances

You'll have more daily details to worry about as your firm expands. You must therefore create a system right away to keep up with everything. To determine what works best for you, test out various organizing techniques, tools, software, and apps. In the end, you are responsible if something is overlooked. Establish organizational procedures that will help you stay on track once you start working full-time.

You must also keep your finances and corporate finances separate. The greatest available alternative for a business checking account is Novo. By consolidating all of your requirements into a single software, you obtain fee-free financial management for your company. Additionally, you can put money aside in Novo Reserves for any other business needs or quarterly taxes.

8. Collaborate with the right people.
Your small business can frequently succeed or fail based on the relationships you build. Choose the ideal associates for your business—people who will support you and are trustworthy. Iron sharpens iron, and this adage also applies to business. Find people that inspire, encourage, and help you develop as a person and business owner, whether they be coworkers, mentors, peers, or friends. Make a two-way roadway as well. Give those in your immediate vicinity the same assistance and support.

9. Make use of your strengths and abilities

In a day, you can only expend so much time and effort. Focus on allocating the majority of your time to the most important business operations. Recognize your advantages and skills, and put them to use. Keep in mind that time is of the essence. By concentrating on your strengths, you'll receive the most value for your money.

10. Contract out your weaknesses

When you first launch your firm, you frequently have to handle every task, regardless of how competent you are at it. Work to outsource jobs as your small business expands and you accumulate more money. These might be your areas of weakness or simply time-consuming duties that prevent you from working on things with more importance. Spend more time on the activities that have the greatest impact, and employ help for the rest.

Chapter 5: How to locate a qualified business mentor.

Every single person requires a mentor at some point in their life. The ultimate aim of business owners is to turn their passion into a profitable enterprise. But achieving that desire is not simple. It requires a lot of effort, and obstacles appear at every turn. Thankfully, business owners don't have to go it alone. Finding the ideal business mentor to help them navigate various stages of development while expanding the business boosts their chances of success.

A mentor is a trusted advisor as well as a coach, guide, tutor, facilitator, and counselor. A mentor is a person who is willing to devote their time and knowledge to helping another person succeed in business or life. An excellent mentor is aware of the importance of being dependable, involved, genuine, and attuned to the requirements of the mentee.

What is a mentor's job description?

For both sides, working with a mentor may be a priceless experience. Both the mentor and the mentee are likely to gain fresh insights into themselves and one another that will aid in their pursuit of professional or corporate objectives. However, for the connection to succeed, each participant must recognize their responsibilities. The mentor role entails a variety of roles;

1. A role model: A successful mentor is someone who is admired and respected for their work in the field they have chosen (business or career). The habits, attitudes, styles, and abilities that the mentor uses and that the mentee wants to imitate and put into practice are frequently sought after by mentees.

2. A Sponsor: Mentors are well-known experts in their field. One of a good mentor's main responsibilities is to open doors for the mentee, suggest alternative business relationships, and actively promote the mentee's company.

3. An Advocate: Effective mentors may decide to engage in activities other than a simple conversation with their mentee. They must purposefully and proactively encourage support for the mentee, influencing and advancing the mentee's standing, skills, and value.

How to locate a reputable business mentor
When you are starting a new business, mentors are essential. They'll aid in your understanding of the field you're in, direct you in what you must do on a personal and professional level to succeed, and frequently just be a listening ear when you need to discuss challenges, triumphs, and concerns.

There are numerous methods for finding a mentor. The most obvious way is through your on- and offline professional network. They could be a buddy, a senior coworker, or a previous boss. Business conventions, seminars, and professional websites like LinkedIn, and Meet-Ups are other resources for finding qualified business mentors.

Qualities of an Effective Mentor

The universe has given us a decent mentor as a gift. If you discover one, make every effort to persuade them that mentoring you is worthwhile. Here are 7 qualities of a good mentor, listed in no particular order:

1. Accessible: There are capable mentors out there. They will always make time for you, no matter how busy they are. When necessary, a good mentor should be reachable via phone, email, or in person.

2. Good Listener: One of the most crucial qualities of a good business mentor is the ability to listen well. By doing this, he or she gives the mentee the tools to explain any issue and organize things.

3. Respectful: Everyone is different, so a good mentor respects the mentee's wishes or opinions and doesn't press too hard when their advice runs counter to the mentee's wishes.

4. Understanding: Good mentors give you space to deal with life's problems because they know that things can go wrong from time to time. They are understanding (to a point).

5. Demanding: Effective mentors force you to step outside of your comfort zone. They realize that change happens when we step outside of our comfort zone.

6. Effective communicators: Effective mentors can explain complex ideas in a language you can understand and stay in touch with you at all times.

7. Likeable: Your mentor must be likable. Someone, you enjoy around making a terrific mentor.

You will eventually require counsel if you are establishing any form of business. However, establishing a mentorship relationship should not be done for its purpose. Write down your business objectives, then consider how a mentor can assist you in achieving them. Describe how you specifically want your mentor to assist you.

Because mentoring can take a lot of time, good mentors are difficult to find. Make sure you are prepared to follow their advice before asking someone to serve as your mentor; otherwise, you will be wasting everyone's time.

Chapter 6: Reasons Why Every Entrepreneur Needs A Mentor, Regardless Of Success

Why do business owners need mentors?
Here are the explanations for why, despite their present successes and accomplishments, I think every business entrepreneur needs a mentor.

1. Mentors offer a new perspective and have more experience.

Mentors have new perspectives that can help solve issues. Everyone's career's most valuable commodity is experiencing, and mentors frequently are aware of the challenges that lie ahead. On your path to success, they can serve as your road map and compass. For instance, my mentor frequently provided me with viewpoints that I hadn't even considered, considerably enhancing my perspective on business and enabling me to avoid failures. This is not to say that I didn't experience my fair share of failures, but because of my mentor's guidance, I was able to advance more quickly rather than make mistakes that could have been avoided.

2. They can aid in your search for more networking opportunities.

Networking is crucial in the world of business. You can take advantage of your mentor to widen your network and open up new prospects.

3. Mentors can help develop the culture of your business.

A company's success or failure can be greatly influenced by its organizational culture. A positive workplace culture keeps employees engaged and motivated. You may establish a culture that upholds the integrity of the company with the assistance of mentors.

4. Assistance in making more decisions is available.

As a manager of a corporation, you may have to make snap judgments that affect the life or death of your company. It feels like walking through a minefield. Your mentor can support you in this situation by guiding you toward the best course of action and minimizing the effects.

5. You can improve your managerial capabilities.

Building a business is challenging, but sustaining it and advancing it is even more challenging. It necessitates a set of management abilities, including problem-solving, communication, planning, and strategic thinking. You can learn these talents with the aid of an excellent mentor.

Everyone needs a mentor (even your mentor).

Mentors are many, but it can take some effort to find a good one. Finding a mentor who works for you is important. You need someone prepared to put up the time and effort necessary for you. Choosing a mentor, in my opinion, is similar to finding a life mate in that you must broaden your network, acquire a sense of your circle, and approach someone you believe reflects your ideals. Utilize sites that match mentorships with students, such as LinkedIn.

Also, keep in mind that mentorships don't always work out. It's alright. Additionally, not all relationships succeed in the end. But the secret is to be clear about what you hope to gain from the mentorship and to have the courage to go for your goals.

Both my mentor and his mentor had mentors before them. With each transfer, the knowledge baton gains strength as it is passed from one generation to the next. When the time is perfect,

I too hope to mentor a young person starting in business in my sector.

Therefore, successful mentoring opens the door to it. The famously used phrase "Your mentors in life are crucial, therefore choose them wisely" attributed to American businessman Robert Kiyosaki captures it perfectly.

www.ingramcontent.com/pod-product-compliance
Lightning Source LLC
Chambersburg PA
CBHW050317220526
45465CB00005B/2033